TEACHER SUPPORT TEAMS IN PRIMARY AND SECONDARY SCHOOLS

Resource Materials for Teachers

Angela Creese
Harry Daniels
Brahm Norwich

David Fulton Publishers
London

David Fulton Publishers Ltd
The Chiswick Centre, 414 Chiswick High Road, London W4 5TF
www.fultonpublishers.co.uk

First published in Great Britain in 1997 by David Fulton Publishers

Note: The rights of Angela Creese, Harry Daniels and Brahm Norwich to be identified as the authors of this work have been asserted by them in accordance with the Copyright, Designs and Patents Act 1988.

David Fulton Publishers is a division of Granada Learning Limited, part of Granada plc.

Copyright © Angela Creese, Harry Daniels and Brahm Norwich

British Library Cataloguing in Publication Data
A catalogue record for this book is available from the British Library.

ISBN 1-85346-484-8

Pages from this book may be photocopied for use only in purchasing institution. Otherwise, all rights reserved. No part of this publication may be reproduced, stored in a retieval system or transmitted, in any form or by any means, electronic, mechanical, photocopying, or otherwise, without the prior permission of the publishers.

Typeset by The Harrington Consultancy Ltd
Printed and bound in Great Britain

Contents

Acknowledgements		v
Part One – Review		1
1	Introduction	1
2	TSTs at a Glance	3
3	Teacher Support Teams – A Description	5
4	Teacher Support Teams in Context	7
Part Two – Putting it into Practice		9
5	Exploring Initial Interest	9
	TST Staff Questionnaire	10
6	Setting up a Teacher Support Team	11
7	Training Sessions	12
	Aims of Training Sessions	13
	How Do Arrangements Work?	14
	Training Session One	
	Timetable	16
	Aims of Training Session One – Presentation 1	17
	Introduction – Presentation 2	18
	Rationale – Presentation 3	19
	Other Similar Schemes – Presentation 4	20
	Brainstorming – Activity 1	21
	Brainstorming – Activity 1, Handout 1	22
	Planning a TST for your School – Activity 2	23
	Planning a TST for your School – Activity 2, Handout 1	24
	Discussion in Cross-School Groups – Activity 3	25
	Discussion in Cross-School Groups – Activity 3, Handout 1	26
	Training Session Two	
	Timetable	28
	TST Simulation Exercise – Activity 4	29
	TST Simulation Exercise – Activity 4, Example 1	33
	TST Simulation Exercise – Activity 4, Example 2	36
	Training Session Three	
	Timetable	40
	TST Simulation Exercise – Activity 5	41
	TST Simulation Exercise – Activity 5, Handout 1	43
	Designing Publicity – Activity 6	44
	An Advertisement – Activity 6, Example 1	45
	Record Keeping for TSTs – Presentation 5	46
	Meeting Record Sheet – Presentation 5, Example 1	47
	Case Record Grid for TST – Presentation 5, Example 2	48
	Evaluating TST Training Sessions – Activity 7	49
	Evaluating the Training Session – Activity 7, Example 1	50
8	Providing Ongoing Support for your TST	52
Appendix – Past Studies		53
	Reading List	57

Acknowledgements

We would like to thank all the teachers involved in the development of TSTs at the 14 schools in which the project was developed. This includes, not only those teachers who were members of the teams themselves, but also all those teachers and administrators who gave their commitment and time to the ideas and procedures involved in setting up, running and evaluating the project.

We would also like to thank Enfield LEA, the Economic and Social Research Council and the DfEE for funding the development and research of Teacher Support Teams in both primary and secondary schools.

PART ONE – REVIEW

Part One reviews the aims and purposes of this book by outlining what TSTs are and how they function. Section 1 contains an introduction to the areas covered in the book. Section 2 offers a preliminary summary of what TSTs are and how they function. Section 3 describes how TSTs are useful in the process of education. Section 4 reviews how TSTs can assist in the changes required of schools under new educational provisions.

1 Introduction

The purpose of this book is to provide resource material for the setting up and development of Teacher Support Teams (TSTs) in schools. It has been designed with the purpose of providing background literature and practical suggestions on what a TST looks like and how it might function. An attempt has been made to make the material relevant to teachers and administrators in both primary and secondary education. Although there are obviously fundamental differences in the organisation of schooling between the primary and secondary sectors, all the material included here was found to be relevant and useful in both contexts. Moreover, readers are encouraged to adapt the material to fit their own needs.

The book is divided into two main parts. Part One aims to describe the rationale behind Teacher Support Teams and reviews previous projects and research. Part Two aims to provide practical tasks and handouts that will be useful in setting up a TST. The tasks and handouts in Part Two were originally part of a three-day training programme at the London University Institute of Education. The original order of presenting the material is retained here so that the reader might have an idea as to how each of the training sessions was organised. Materials are listed under Training Sessions 1, 2 and 3. Each training session is organised chronologically and a time frame is given for each activity. This is in order to stress that, although activities can be used independently, they were originally conceptualised as being interrelated and part of an ongoing training package.

At this point we would wish to draw attention to our understanding of TST training and the role of TST trainers. We see TST training as a process through which schools may develop their own response to a small set of key concepts and thereby start to build their own version of the TST idea in their own schools. The facilitators of TST training sessions need not necessarily be experts on TSTs. However, we feel that it is important that they should be well prepared for the activity and familiar with the background information. Most activities involve discussion among TST members from the same school and across schools. Usually, after small group discussions, the whole group is brought together at the end of the session to share and compare ideas. The facilitation of this process is the session leader's main role. The management of discussion by the facilitator will involve the need to question, explain, draw out arguments and points of view, clarify and summarise.

Evaluation as part of the process of establishing a TST is also considered in Part Two. Activities covered in the training sessions are open to evaluation and an evaluation document is included as an example. Suggestions as to how TST members can evaluate their own work are also included.

2 TSTs at a Glance

What are TSTs?

- They may be seen to constitute a practical embodiment of a school's commitment to SEN by offering an indirect mechanism for supporting pupils, through supporting teachers in a setting in which knowledge and understanding may be shared and developed with professional peers.
- While other professional groups have been using systems for peer professional support and consultation, teachers who have considerable knowledge and skill rarely share this with colleagues. TSTs set up a forum for professional educators to share, manage and solve problems which arise from teachers' individual and immediate classroom concerns.
- In seeking assistance, teachers make requests to the team who help them to define the problem(s), consider possible alternatives and try out practical strategies.
- In that TSTs develop structured approaches to collaborative problem-solving with an emphasis on follow-up and review, they differ from much of the informal peer support which is to be found in many schools. Teachers may often ask each other for advice. However, these exchanges typically take place in the context of busy staff rooms in a very short space of time and rarely with any possibility of reviewing the effects of the advice. TSTs allocate a dedicated amount of time to a referring teacher, in a calm and peaceful setting in which issues may be discussed without interruption and in confidence.
- Crucially they embody the problem-solving cycle in that teachers are offered the opportunity to monitor and review the situation through follow-up meetings.

How do TSTs Work?

- Typically three classroom teachers serve as the core team, who call on outside support and advisory staff and parents when needed.
- Teams meet weekly or fortnightly with the teacher making a request for support – meetings last about 45 minutes (usually during lunchtime or after school). A team member usually collects relevant information about the teacher's concern before the meeting.
- Typically one case is dealt with per meeting – either a new request or a follow-up. Unless a case is closed a follow-up date is always agreed at

which the situation will be reviewed.
- Teams keep confidential notes about cases to enable follow-up work and a log of meetings.
- Teachers involved in meetings need to have some time release from other responsibilities.
- The principles and practical aspects of TSTs need staff and headteacher support.

3 Teacher Support Teams – A Description

We originally conceived of TSTs as a system of support from a team of peers for class teachers experiencing teaching difficulties in relation to special educational needs (SEN). Our model was that individual teachers request support on a voluntary basis from a team which usually includes the SEN coordinator, a senior teacher and another class teacher. The team, along with the referring teacher, collaborate in order to understand the problem(s) and design appropriate forms of intervention related to learning and behaviour difficulties. Our own research suggests that TSTs actually function in a much broader way than we originally thought would be the case. In some schools they may well function as supports for teachers' problem-solving far beyond the original SEN remit.

Something for Teachers

TSTs are novel in that they are an example of a school-based development designed to give support and assistance to individual teachers. In this way, TSTs address a significant but neglected area of school development which has the potential to enhance the working conditions of teachers. They involve a sharing of expertise between colleagues, rather than some teachers acting as experts to others.

Many classroom teachers feel that they do not have sufficient training and support to meet many of the challenges presented by children with SEN in their classes. They tend to lack confidence in their ability to provide programmes of study which are appropriately differentiated. They find themselves working in school situations where they regularly teach large classes with insufficient internal special needs support and where external resources are rarely available. Facing the task of meeting a wide range of needs in isolation can lead to acute stress or disaffection. This can happen to any teacher working in unfavourable circumstances. Many teachers may also wish to seek peer support for resolving problems that they experience in the general life of their classrooms and schools. They may wish to complement or supplement their own and their schools' ways of solving problems through reference to a TST.

TSTs aim to enable staff to develop their confidence and competence in making provision for children with SEN in mainstream classes. They provide a forum for teachers to share teaching knowledge and skill, and to express and receive collegial and emotional support. In this way TSTs can also enable teachers to learn specific methods and have access to different teaching approaches. They also help teachers to realise that they are not alone and that others have similar difficulties. Teams also provide teachers with an opportunity to air frustrations around disheartening behavioural issues.

Something for Schools

The principle of TSTs is based on making the most of the knowledge and skills of teachers already in a school. In this way they may be seen to complement existing forms of SEN work within schools and existing patterns of informal mutual peer support as and when they exist. The development of practices of integration of children with special educational needs has been associated with a gradual acceptance that assessment and intervention must focus not only on individual difficulties but also on factors within schools which can prevent or exacerbate problems (NCC, 1989). In this way, TSTs are an intermediary form of provision between individual child-focused support arrangements and whole-school policy initiatives. Schools need to find new and effective schemes to develop their internal support for SEN and the implementation of the Code of Practice (DfE, 1994), and TSTs provide one such scheme.

Something for Children

If teachers do not feel that they are achieving their aims, and if they become demotivated and frustrated, the children in their classes are unlikely to experience the same quality of teaching as when their teachers feel that they are able to engage with the demands of teaching and tolerate the pressures that the task exerts. The massive changes that teachers have experienced recently, along with the increase in diversity of their pupils' needs, mean that teachers are having to adapt in many different ways. If teachers can share and assist one another in these circumstances, they are likely to feel more relaxed and positive about their teaching.

Something for Everyone

TSTs serve to support teachers through school-based problem-solving groups which function to support pupils indirectly through teacher collaboration. They provide a facility for teachers to exchange ideas, air feelings and work on problem-solving issues relating to teachers' work in the classroom. There are many ways to improve the educational opportunities for children with special educational needs. TSTs can be seen as one of them. Thus, TSTs have characteristics in common with various other support schemes, while offering a distinct form of support directly to the teacher. TSTs are similar to the following schemes:

- whole-staff review and support meetings for pupils with SEN
- teacher pairings for mutual support
- external consultant support to groups of teachers
- external consultant support to individual teachers
- internal support (SEN coordinator to individual teachers)
- LEA personal counselling service for teachers.

4 Teacher Support Teams in Context

Coping with Change

The last ten years have witnessed great changes in the organisation of schooling. Whatever the source of these changes, their implementation has fallen, to a great extent, on the teachers themselves. This has often meant that teachers are dealing with higher levels of dilemma and tension both in and out of the classroom, as they endeavour to deliver the curriculum in ways which are relevant and meaningful to the diverse needs of their pupils. Teachers are only too aware of the tensions and the lonely and stressful experience that such changes may bring. Moreover, tired, anxious teachers are unlikely to be able to implement these changes effectively. This has obvious implications for their pupils.

Making a Change

In recent years there has been a movement away from excluding groups of children from mainstream classes. Criticism of the overuse of 'pull-out' or withdrawal for pupils with SEN has given way, increasingly, to an acknowledgement of the benefits of an inclusive education in the mainstream. The development of TSTs needs to be seen in the context of these moves. The teaching of more children with SEN in ordinary schools and the recognition of whole-school approaches to SEN have been backed up by government legislation and reports (DES, 1989; NCC, 1989; ILEA, 1985; Galloway, 1985).

These developments have special relevance to schools now with the requirement in the Education Act 1993 and its associated Code of Practice (DfE, 1994) that schools specify and publish their SEN policies and practices. The concept of TSTs in particular was recommended by the Elton Report (DES, 1989). The support such teams offer is also consistent with Stages 1 and 2 of the assessment process as set out in the Code of Practice. It is envisaged that the presence of TSTs would enable more effective linking with outside services and prioritising of need at Stage 3.

The principles behind inclusive education have been welcomed by many teachers. However, it is important to recognise that the practicalities of adapting classrooms to be accessible for learning to take place for all pupils, has fallen mostly on class teachers. Moreover, these changes are expected to occur in times of cutbacks in support and resources. Increased levels of stress resulting from change can exacerbate feelings of loneliness and isolation. At such times, teachers need stronger support structures rather than weaker ones. TSTs are to be seen as providing teachers with collegial assistance in making these changes. Thus, the rationale for TSTs can be summarised as follows:

- a forum for educators to share knowledge and skill with each other;
- a school resource for supporting teachers and, through this, enhancing provision for children, especially those with SEN;
- a practical embodiment of a school's whole-school commitment and policy for SEN;
- an opportunity for teachers to learn specific methods and have access to different curricula material.

Applying the Research

The resource material available in this book is based on the successful setting up of TSTs, and evaluation of several pieces of research. A full report on the research projects which have contributed to the development work can be found in the Appendix along with a reading list for further reading. The schools involved in these projects range from inner-city London schools to rural county schools. Success in such a variety of schools supports the belief that the type of assistance TSTs provide is relevant to teachers in any context.

PART TWO – PUTTING IT INTO PRACTICE

5 Exploring Initial Interest

Part Two consists of four sections. Section 5 is concerned with exploring a school's initial interest in the ideas behind a TST. Section 6 looks at the setting up of a TST. Section 7 offers an outline and examples of how staff can be trained in the setting up and running of a TST. Section 8 suggests how to provide ongoing support for the TST.

Investigating whether a school feels it needs, and would benefit from, a TST is an important first stage in establishing a TST.

A school may be interested in exploring the idea of TST for a number of reasons. It may be the case, for example, that it is relevant to other INSET concerns a school may have, such as SEN provisions or developing behaviour management. Initial interest could be explored through a half day INSET activity in which the materials found in Training Session One (pages 15 to 26) could be used in an adapted form. The Training Session One Presentations most relevant are:

Presentation 1 – Modified aims
Presentation 2 – Introduction
Presentation 3 – Rationale
Presentation 4 – Other similar schemes
Activity 1 and Activity 1, Handout 1 – Brainstorming.

In addition, it would be necessary to plan an activity relevant to the school's situation and to use the outcomes of the Brainstorming Activity to evaluate the potential use of TSTs in the school. Should INSET generate staff curiosity, this could be followed up by a questionnaire to all staff eliciting their interest in more detail. An example of a TST Staff Questionnaire is shown overleaf.

TST Staff Questionnaire

1 When you have had concerns about the teaching or learning of pupils or pupils with special educational needs, what kinds of assistance or support have there been for you?

- informally from a colleague ☐ *(tick)*
- from head of department ☐
- from head of year ☐
- from SEN/Learning Support coordinator ☐

2 A teacher support team (TST) is a team of 3 to 4 teachers, including the SEN coordinator, which can provide initial and follow-up support to teachers who request this support on a voluntary and confidential basis. It is a forum for exchanging ideas, airing feelings and problem-solving.

a Would you have a need for such a team in your school?

Yes ☐ Not sure ☐ No ☐

Can you explain your answer_____
_____
_____
_____

3 a Would you be willing in principle to request support from such a team?

Yes ☐ Not sure ☐ No ☐

b What kinds of issues or problems might you refer to the team?_____
_____
_____
_____

c What would be an appropriate team size? (circle one number)

3 4 5 other

4 Who would be suitable team members (in terms of their teaching position)?
_____
_____
_____
_____

6 Setting up a Teacher Support Team

Who is doing it?

Before a school starts formal training, a decision needs to be made about who will guide the sessions. This is likely to be either:

- somebody with previous experience in TSTs;
- an enthusiastic individual or group of individuals who have not had any previous experience but who are willing to take responsibility for familiarising themselves with the practice and leading the training sessions; or,
- an outside agent such as a consultant from the support services or from an institute of higher education.

The information which follows is designed to facilitate whichever of the above routes is chosen in setting up a TST.

Initial Groundwork

Several factors seem to be important in developing collaborative schemes in general, and TSTs in particular:

- a catalyst, in the form of a member of senior management, who floats the idea among colleagues;
- extra resources – initially in the form of time off from teaching duties to train members of the TST and continuing support in the form of cover for referring teachers;
- a level of trust among the participants, both within the team and outside, in the sense that it is crucial that TST members are respected by the large majority of the teaching staff and have the full support of senior management.

Setting up TSTs depends on clear and detailed initial communications and negotiations between the schools and those with the development ideas and training resources. This involves the heads and the whole staff in understanding what is involved, considering what the TST arrangement has to offer the school and then deciding to commit the school and their resources to enable TSTs to work. If they are to function successfully, TSTs need to be designed to fit the needs of the schools as perceived by the TST team and their colleagues.

7 Training Sessions

A training period for TST members is an important part of setting up a team. A variety of issues needs to be covered, from the fine details like who makes the tea during a referral session, to larger issues such as how to give helpful suggestions to referring teachers.

Materials and Activities

The training sessions described here were held on three separate days over a period of four months. They were used in the first instance with primary schools and in the second with secondary schools. On each occasion they were backed by two trainers from a university. Over the course of the training periods, fourteen schools (eight primary and six secondary) sent potential TST members. There were usually three or four teachers from each school. Activities were designed to allow teachers both to work together in their own school teams and to collaborate with colleagues from other schools in cross-team tasks. The programme included presentations, and whole-group and small-group activities ranging from brainstorming to problem-solving tasks.

What follows is a version of this training programme. This is offered as one of many possible ways of organising the training period. Trainers are encouraged to arrive at their own configurations. However, it is suggested that time *between* the training sessions is given for each TST to negotiate the various arrangements within their schools which will need to be made for the team to operate. For example, the process of consultation with the school management team and the rest of the staff needs careful consideration.

The material for the training days is organised in the following way.

Timetables For each of the three training sessions a timetable of events is given. These do not need to be followed in a prescriptive manner. They are used here to organise the material.

Presentations These can be used as overhead-projector presentations or handouts. The session facilitator should use them to generate discussions and cover main points.

Activities These are done as a whole group, in small groups and in pairs. With each activity there is a list of instructions and often some additional material given as a handout. Each activity is organised in the same way: aims, time, organisation and procedures.

Handouts and Examples In addition to the instructions for each activity there may be a handout and/or example to go with the activity.

For a full list of presentations, activities, handouts and examples, see the contents page at the front of this book.

Aims of Training Sessions

Preparing a school for a TST involves enabling participating teachers to:

- be familiar with the concepts and principles of school-based teacher support teams, as providing proper support *and* meeting special educational needs

- understand the function, risks and constraints of designing and running teacher support teams

- design an appropriate teacher support team for their school through consultation with colleagues

- be aware of and sensitive to the needs and feelings of the teacher making requests for support

- be proficient in
  - receiving requests for support
  - conducting meetings
  - liaising with parents and support services
  - making sense of teaching problems
  - devising appropriate forms of advice
  - assessing outcomes in the classroom
  - reviewing and evaluating the overall TST arrangement.

How Do Arrangements Work?

When a TST is being planned in a school there are a number of issues which need to be resolved. The following list may serve as an aide mémoire.

- Who is the target population?
- Who can refer to the team?
  - some schools may wish to extend the TST principle to all staff, including classroom assistants.
- Who serves on the team and how are they to be identified?
- Who coordinates the team?
- How many referrals may be handled at one meeting?
- How and when should meetings be conducted?
- How best can TSTs make use of:
  - psychologists
  - parents
  - advisory teachers
  - support services?
- How to make recommendations and gain access to resources?
- How to design recording sheets that minimise the amount of recording?
- How to follow-up recommendations?
- How to support and encourage team use?
- How to review and evaluate the team process (formative)?
  - adapting team procedures.

Training Session One

Training Session One – Timetable

Introduction (30 minutes)
  Teacher Support Teams
  Aims
  Rationale of TSTs
  Similarities to Other Schemes

Presentation from an experienced team member – a Guest Speaker (20 minutes)
  A descriptive account of what it feels like to work in a TST and the benefits for the school, teachers and children.

Break

Your initial impressions of TSTs (45 minutes)
  – a group brainstorming activity

Analysis of operational issues in setting up TSTs in your school
  – matters needing attention

Break

Planning the setting up of TSTs in your schools
  – own school group (45 minutes)
  – cross-school groups (45 minutes)

Identifying tasks for next session (30 minutes)

End

Aims of Training Session One
Presentation 1

Aims:

1 To become familiar with the concepts and principles of school-based support teams as providing peer support and meeting special educational needs.

2 To design a TST relevant to the needs of the school, based on an understanding of the operational issues and through staff consultation.

3 To develop knowledge and skills in offering sensitive and practical support in the teams.

Introduction – Presentation 2

TSTs involve a school-based development

- in which the school provides support and assistance to individual teachers

- through a group of teachers

- who work with individual colleagues

- who request support on a voluntary basis

- to solve, manage or ease teaching problems.

Rationale – Presentation 3

The rationale of TSTs is:

1 A forum for educators to share knowledge and skill with each other.

2 A school resource for supporting teachers and through this, provision for children, especially those with SEN.

3 A practical embodiment of a school's whole-school commitment and policy for SEN.

4 An opportunity for teachers to learn specific methods and have access to different teaching materials.

Other Similar Schemes – Presentation 4

1 Whole-staff review and support meeting for pupils with SEN.

2 Teacher pairings for mutual support.

3 External consultant support to group of teachers.

4 External consultant support to individual teachers.

5 Internal support (SEN coordinator to individual teachers).

6 LEA personal counselling service for teachers.

Brainstorming – Activity 1

Aims　　　　　To think about the strengths/weaknesses/opportunities/threats of a TST

Organisation　Pairs or small groups

Time　　　　10 minutes

Procedure
1. Ask teachers to brainstorm what they think the strengths/weaknesses/opportunities/threats of a TST might be for the children, teachers and management in the school in which they work.

2. The session facilitator writes this on the board, allowing for discussion.

3. Give the group Activity 1, Handout 1 as a summary.

Brainstorming – Activity 1, Handout 1
Initial Impressions of TST Members – Summary

Strengths
- teachers helping each other
- understanding what others think
- fairly immediate help
- chance to do something practical – not always found with outside support
- workable solutions appropriate to particular school
- some privacy about your teaching problems
- with less external support, and schools more autonomous, schools can offer internal support

Weaknesses
- is there enough time because of other commitments?
- teachers may be reluctant to say they have teaching problems
- can requests for support be kept confidential?
- teachers already support one another
- so much change happening already – what future for TSTs?

Opportunities
- can focus on children's difficulties rather than teachers' problems
- sharing techniques with others
- schools can offer internal support – now that schools becoming more autonomous and less external support available
- could be better prepared for recent changes such as less external support

Threats
- requests for support may be seen as sign of weakness and used against people in redundancy decisions
- so much change happening to schools so don't know the future of TSTs
- general atmosphere of threat at present and lack of job security

Planning a TST for your School Activity 2

Aim	To plan the TST for your school in your own school group
Organisation	Teachers work in school-group teams
Time	45 minutes
Procedure	1 Consult the list of matters needing consideration (see Activity 1, Handout 1) to identify those which you have considered already in your schools. – Are there further matters to consider relating to your particular circumstances (e.g. split site, number of teams)? – What decisions have you made already? 2 Looking again at the list provided, what matters do you still need to consider? – Discuss what is needed to make decisions about these matters? – Who needs to be consulted in your school and what strategies would you use?

Planning a TST for your School
Activity 2, Handout 1

Matters needing consideration
- who can request support?
- about what problems?
- who serves on the team?
- rotation of membership
- how are requests to be received?
- timing of TST meetings
- who coordinates meetings?
- making recommendations to requesting teacher
- follow-up meetings with requesting teacher
- making use of others: parents; external support services
- coordinating and overlapping with other support services
- recording of proceedings and outcomes; confidentiality
- publicising TST; encouraging its use
- evaluating processes and outcomes; adapting/changing in response.

Discussion in Cross-School Groups
Activity 3

Aim	Cross-school groups
Organisation	Two TSTs from different schools
Time	30 minutes
Procedure	1 Present a synopsis of your TST situation to another school group.
	2 Explain
	– what you have planned so far and why
	– the further considerations you face
	– any problems and possible strategies.
	3 The role of the listening group is to
	– question and probe the emergent TST plan
	– make suggestions about the plan and strategy.

Discussion in Cross-School Groups
Activity 3, Handout 1

1 Present a synopsis of your TST situation to another school group.

2 Explain
- what you have planned so far and why
- the further considerations you face
- any problems and possible strategies.

3 The role of the listening group is to
- question and probe the emergent TST plan
- make suggestions about the plan and strategy.

Training Session Two

Training Session Two – Timetable

Report back from schools on TST setting up processes (90 minutes)

Break

Simulation of TST in operation with case studies from your schools (75 minutes)

Break

Simulations continued (120 minutes)

    Discussion of simulations

Planning for next session, including documentation for running TSTs (45 minutes)

TST Simulation Exercise – Activity 4

Aims	To enable you to gain insights into the processes of supporting teachers with their concerns about teaching pupils with special educational needs. To assist you in developing skills and knowledge involved in running a support team.
Organisation	School teams
Time	1 hour
Procedure	You will be working in school groups

1 Before starting the role play read **Issues in running a TST** (see page 31).

2 Now in your school groups decide on which person will act as the requesting teacher. The others act as TST teachers.

3 The TST team will probably need a few minutes to decide amongst themselves how they wish to run the meeting.

4 During this time the requesting teacher can finalise how to present the concerns or problems.

5 **Debriefing – after 30 minutes:**
   – Get out of your roles by each person taking a turn to say how it felt to take part in the simulation.
   – Then you can begin to consider the process of supporting and the kinds of outcomes arrived at.

These are some questions to consider in discussing the simulation

A Sensitivity
- How was the requesting teacher put at ease?
- What signs did the group give of accurate listening and empathy?

B Identifying the problem
- With what evidence was the problem identified?
- To what extent has the identified problem been related to other problems?
- To what extent has the problem been identified clearly and specifically?

C Analysis
- How has the problem been accounted for in terms of the individual, group, class and school?
- Was reference made to more than one of these factors?

D Action advised
- What kind of action was advised?
- Did advice relate to more than one of the four factors under **C** above (i.e. the individual, group, class and school)?
- Was there any discussion about follow-up procedures?
- As a group, record five main points which summarise what you got out of doing the simulation.

Issues in running a TST

1. **Joint function of support teams**
   - Assisting teachers to find positive and feasible ways forward while recognising what they can expect to be responsible for in the circumstances.
   - Providing reassurance and emotional support to teachers.

This means that attention needs to be given to showing sensitivity and empathy by listening and not being overly prescriptive and directive. Consider:

- How can you put the requesting teacher at ease?
- What would you do to listen accurately to what the teacher is saying directly and showing indirectly?

You need to consider also what balance you will strike between **providing** your assessment and advice about action and **enabling** the requesting teacher to rediscover and work out their own ideas and plans.

2. **Using an action planning schema**

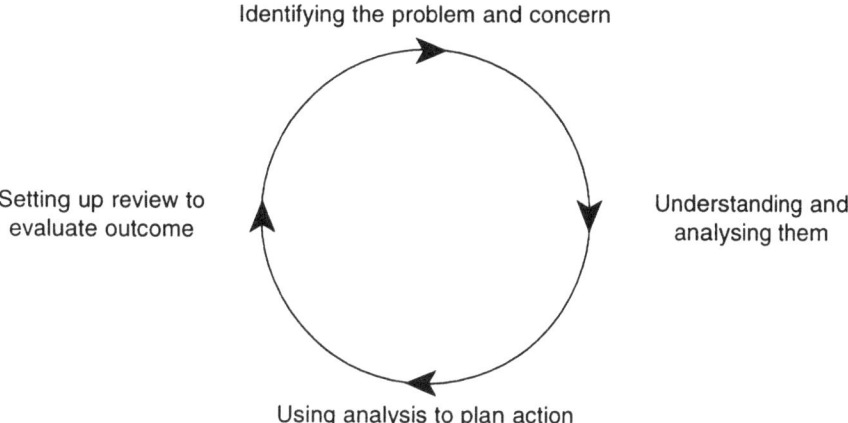

This schema can be used in planning for individual, group, class or school-level action.

3 **Identifying the problems and concerns**
   - What evidence is being used to identify problems and concerns?
   - Have identified problems been related to other problems?
   - To what extent has the problem been identified clearly and specifically?
   - What else needs to be done to clarify the situation in the longer term?

4 **Understanding and analysing the problems**
   - What knowledge can the requesting teacher and you bring to understanding and analysing the problems?
   - Are you considering factors at individual, class, school and family levels?
   - Are you considering strengths and weaknesses?
   - Are you and the requesting teacher able to analyse the problem – how does this come about (in a way which can lead to some action to improve matters)?

5 **Using analysis to plan action**
   - Can you and the requesting teacher use the understanding and analysis to plan feasible action?
   - Have you made full use of existing strengths in the pupil and his or her situation?
   - If you have more than one possible action plan, how will you decide which to use? What will be your priorities and why?
   - Have you considered what materials and other support are needed to carry out the plan?
   - Have you considered the length of time before you review the case again?

TST Simulation Exercise Activity 4, Example 1

Examples 1 and 2 were written by teachers prior to Training Session Two in preparation for the simulation activity (Activity 4). They are given here, not only to capture the pressures of classroom life through the use of the teacher's voice, but also to show two kinds of situations in which the TST could support teachers. The first Example describes a whole-class problem, while the second describes issues related to an individual child's needs.

Case Study of a Classroom Problem

Background
The class consists of 18 pupils: 10 boys, 8 girls
The teacher sees the class for five one hour lessons a week
The subject is Science, the class is the bottom set

   Monday, Period 2
   Tuesday, Period 4
   Wednesday, Period 5
   Thursday, Period 5
   Friday, Period 2

Generally speaking, the Monday and Friday mid-morning lessons are better than the later periods on the other days.

Class strengths and weaknesses
Strengths
- there is good quality work on display from everyone in the classroom
- class produced excellent project work, when it was hammered home that this was for GCSE.

Weaknesses
- zero motivation; negative ethos, in general
- academically there is a huge spread which includes
  - pupils who have problems writing a sentence
  - pupils who have specific learning difficulties
  - academically average, but disaffected pupils
  - two pupils who are more able, both with literacy and general learning skills

- consistently aggressive, uncooperative behaviour from seven pupils who, variously, have outside agency involvement (Social Services, counselling, police)
- significant emotional/behavioural difficulties which leads to some cooling-off and/or formal exclusion period
- so many dynamics in the group; their unpredictability is the most stressful feature
- mood swings, not sulks or silences, but mood swings that you know all about
- they bring all their problems and relationships into the classroom: they can't, or won't, leave these outside the classroom door (e.g. if they have a row in Maths, this continues in Science)
- pupils will only engage in what they have been asked to do if they are happy with the task – if not, they are impossible to teach
- lack of self-confidence/self-esteem; pupils call themselves 'The Units'.

When observed by a colleague – they're my worst group, too, except you've got more of them.

Learning environment
- bottom set Science
- unpredictable behaviour and attendance rates
- ability range, though predominantly disaffected, with learning difficulties
- enthusiastic teacher, fairly new to teaching, whose general approach is calm, clear, and encouraging; this is her most daunting class.

Problem as perceived by the teacher
See comments under **Class weaknesses** and **Learning environment**
- range of ability/difficulties
- predominance of disaffection
- frequent 'acting out' behaviour
- low motivation levels
- unpredictability
- erratic attendance
- over exposure to subject (an hour a day); difficulty in sustaining pupil and teacher motivation
- afternoon lessons the worst
- Science seen as a very hard subject by pupils

- heavy content; 'sometimes seems like packages of stuff that we have to hurl at them'
- setting; same pupils see a lot of one another in Maths, French, and Science
- lack of confidence in own abilities; even the two more able (potential grade D) were surprised when told this.

Interventions so far
- support has been offered at various times by SEN coordinator and senior teacher (to support pupils with behavioural difficulties and pupils with Statements) and by welfare assistant (for pupils with emotional/behavioural difficulties)
- at one stage, all three were involved, once a week; this was seen as the most successful time due in part to the withdrawal of two pupils!
- support was not always responded to positively by pupils; ironically it was often better received by the non-targeted pupils
- when doing open-ended research and using the computers, support was better received
- some support staff lacked subject specialism and therefore credibility in some pupils' eyes
- support was not possible for all lessons; lack of continuity was a weakness
- support in a withdrawal situation for two of the more difficult pupils eventually worked well, with some carry-over of more responsible behaviour into the class, but this was not consistent: there were attempts at a behaviour and learning contract
- report card to monitor behaviour of certain pupils
- Head of Department would sometimes look after pupils in his room
- curriculum modification: 'If this was the only class I had to prepare for, and when I've spent all night on the computer doing some cutting and sticking activities, we could have a much better time of it' (Science teacher).

Personnel involved
As above, support staff, plus outside agency involvement, plus Deputy Head (in support of behaviour contract).

TST Simulation Exercise
Activity 4, Example 2

Case Study of an Individual Child's Needs

Background
Year 8 pupil. Not statemented. Likely soon to be identified as Level 2 on SEN Code of Practice.

Classroom strengths and weaknesses
Strengths
- basic literacy skills
- neat presentation
- enjoys drawing and draws well
- in a good mood can be enthusiastic and sociable with a nice smile
- regular attendance
- generally well-equipped with pens, pencil, record book, etc.
- most homework completed
- always looks neat and tidy.

Weaknesses
- lack of self-control, immature
- very moody, prone to sulk
- disruptive behaviour and sometimes very aggressive behaviour both to peers and adults: on one occasion he got out of his seat and walked to the front of the class to attack another pupil; this was while the class teacher was talking to the class and there were two support teachers in the room
- feels he is always being 'picked on'
- limited achievement with in-class tasks, very demanding of attention
- very poor spelling of which he is very self-conscious
- heavy reliance on confident girl who gives him reassurance
- talks very quickly.

Learning environment
- mixed ability tutor group
- taught in different classrooms, three hours a week
- generally one and sometimes two support teachers work with the class teacher as there are three statemented pupils with severe learning difficulties and at least another six with some literacy difficulties
- there is always work displayed on the classroom walls: despite the

fact that they work in three different rooms there is usually work from the class in each room – the pupil concerned does have examples of his work on display
- the class is disruptive and volatile, with a number of immature pupils
- the atmosphere is often noisy, chatty, and undisciplined, with a general lack of respect for each other as individuals
- the class is unpredictable in its response to different learning situations: no matter how much preparation has been done, a lesson can be destroyed in a matter of minutes; yet on other occasions, a lesson prepared in seconds off the top of the head can work well.

Problem as perceived by the teacher
- often won't settle and demands constant attention which makes it difficult to concentrate on the rest of the class
- can be volatile/violent when thwarted or disagreed with; this can destroy the learning environment in seconds: rest of the class over react to the disruption caused and react by joining in or starting their own disruption
- he has a poor self-image and therefore needs praise and reassurance but will not always respond to it
- satisfying his needs means that other pupils do not always get attention when they need it.

Intervention so far
By the teacher
- positive encouragement
- concentration on successes and limiting activities which he will find difficult
- trying to take interest in him as an individual, asking about hobbies, etc.
- asking to leave the room for 'cooling off' period
- referring to Year Head and Deputy Head.

By the school
- change of class
- report cards to monitor daily behaviour
- discussions with mother.

Personnel involved
Year Head, Deputy Head, Learning Support Department.

Training Session Three

Training Session Three – Timetable

Report back about setting up and running TSTs (75 minutes)

Simulation (75 minutes)

Break

Finalising materials and procedures (30 minutes)

    Publicity
    Materials
    Evaluating the team

Evaluating the training period (10 minutes)

TST Simulation Exercise – Activity 5

Aims
To give further practice in simulating a TST. This activity is the same as that used in Training Session Two but teachers work in **cross-school groups** instead of their own school groups.
To enable you to gain some insights into the processes of supporting teachers with their concerns about teaching pupils with SEN.
To assist you in developing skills and knowledge involved in running a support team.

Organisation Cross-school teams

Time 1½ hours

Procedure You will be working in cross-school groups
1 Before starting the role play remind yourself of the **Issues in running a TST** (page 31).
2 One person from School A will act as the requesting teacher and the teachers from School B as the TST team.
3 The TST team will probably need a few minutes to decide amongst themselves how they wish to run the meeting.
4 During this time the requesting teacher can finalise how to present the concern/s or problem/s.
5 The other members from School A to act as observers.
6 One of the observers to assume the role of coordinator of the simulation.

After 10 minutes
– The coordinator suspends the simulation for not more than 10 minutes and asks each person, including participants and observers, to give a brief descriptive account of what they consider has been happening.
– After this, the simulation should be resumed and allowed to reach a conclusion.

7 **Debriefing – after 30 minutes:**
– Get out of your roles by each person taking a turn to say how it felt to take part in the simulation.
– Then you can begin to consider the process of supporting and the kinds of outcomes arrived at.

These are some questions to consider in discussing the simulation

A Sensitivity
– How was the requesting teacher put at ease?
– What signs did the group give of accurate listening and empathy?

B Identifying the problem
- With what evidence was the problem identified?
- To what extent has the identified problem been related to other problems?
- To what extent has the problem been identified clearly and specifically?

C Analysis
- How has the problem been accounted for in terms of the individual, group, class and school?
- Was reference made to more than one of these factors?

D Action advised
- What kind of action was advised?
- Did advice relate to more than one of the four factors under **C** above (i.e. the individual, group, class and school)?
- Was there any discussion about follow-up procedures?
- As a group, record five main points which summarise what you got out of the simulation.

TST Simulation Exercise
Activity 5, Handout 1

You will be working in cross-school groups
1. Before starting the role play remind yourself of the **Issues in running a TST** (page 31).
2. One person from School A will act as the requesting teacher and the teachers from School B as the TST team.
3. The TST team will probably need a few minutes to decide amongst themselves how they wish to run the meeting.
4. During this time the requesting teacher can finalise how to present the concern/s or problem/s.
5. The other members from School A to act as observers.
6. One of the observers to assume the role of coordinator of the simulation.

After 10 minutes
- The coordinator suspends the simulation for not more than 10 minutes and asks each person, including participants and observers, to give a brief descriptive account of what they consider has been happening.
- After this, the simulation should be resumed and allowed to reach a conclusion.

7. **Debriefing – after 30 minutes:**
   - Get out of your roles by each person taking a turn to say how it felt to take part in the simulation.
   - Then you can begin to consider the process of supporting and the kinds of outcomes arrived at.

These are some questions to consider in discussing the simulation

A Sensitivity
- How was the requesting teacher put at ease?
- What signs did the group give of accurate listening and empathy?

B Identifying the problem
- With what evidence was the problem identified?
- To what extent has the identified problem been related to other problems?
- To what extent has the problem been identified clearly and specifically?

C Analysis
- How has the problem been accounted for in terms of the individual, group, class and school?
- Was reference made to more than one of these factors?

D Action advised
- What kind of action was advised?
- Did advice relate to more than one of the four factors under **C** above (i.e. the individual, group, class and school)?
- Was there any discussion about follow-up procedures?
- As a group, record five main points which summarise what you got out of the simulation.

Designing Publicity – Activity 6

Aims	To identify who needs to know about the TST, what they need to know and how to inform them
Organisation	School TST group activity
Time	20 minutes
Procedure	1 In school groups teachers brainstorm issues relating to the publicity of their TST.
	2 School groups exchange this information with others in discussion.

An Advertisement
Activity 6, Example 1

What is a TST?
The TST is a new venture, providing support and assistance to members of staff in dealing with the range of learning and behavioural difficulties of pupils, or groups of pupils, which may be encountered.

What will the TST do?
Staff seeking help will make requests to the team. The team will help the member of staff define the problem(s), consider possible alternatives and try out practical strategies. Follow-up meetings will be offered to review progress and give further support if appropriate.

How will the TST operate?
The team consists of three members

    John Smith
    Jane Brown
    Susan White

and will be available every Tuesday after school.

Members of staff will book meetings with the team via Jane Brown, who is the diary secretary, or they may speak to any other team member who will pass their request to Jane.

It is expected that meetings will last approximately 30 minutes. Tea and biscuits will be served! Meetings will take place in Susan White's office.

All meetings are completely confidential and will take the form of an informal discussion where problems are shared and worked through together. Records will be kept to assist follow-up and as part of the London Institute's research project, but individual staff will not be identifiable to anyone outside the team.

The TST is not
– a personal counselling service
– a group of know-alls
– a covert form of appraisal.

The TST is
– a forum for staff to share expertise and understanding.

If you have any further questions, please talk to one of the team members.

Record Keeping for TSTs
Presentation 5

MATERIALS needed for Recording TST Meetings

1 Meeting record – to cover each meeting
- when – the date, time start and end
- who present
- number of cases dealt with
- if meeting cancelled.

2 Case record – summary of each case
- teacher name, code, initials, date
- nature of presenting request
- name of pupil and class
- understanding and analysis of situation
- action taken or recommended
- follow up date set
- any other details.

Meeting Record Sheet
Presentation 5, Example 1

TST Meeting Record Sheet

CONFIDENTIAL

Date *16/11/96*   Ref. No. *001*

Time Start *9.10 am*

Statement of discussion/focus

1. *To establish sympathy with colleagues regarding working environment.*
2. *Discussing/compromising with colleague in question about the possibility of displaying work.*
3. *To negotiate storage space within classroom.*

Information gained from research

Strategies

Building a positive relationship with colleague for long term co-operation.
Anticipating problems and applying yourself practically.
Approaching colleague about putting up display work.

Time ended *10 am*

Date of next meeting *A.S.A.P (30/1/97)?*

Case Record Grid for TST Presentation 5, Example 2

School Name: _____

Date: _____ **Record Sheet Number:** _____ **of** _____

Child Number: _____

Date of referral	
Pupil age	
Pupil gender	
Class	
Teacher initials and gender	
Number of follow-ups	
Case closed or open	
Kind of difficulty referred	
Forms of support offered	
Others consulted	
Outcome of advice	

Evaluating TST Training Sessions
Activity 7

Aim To evaluate the TST Training Sessions

Organisation Individually

Time 10 minutes

Procedure
1 Teachers spend 10 minutes evaluating the training sessions.
2 These are collected and used as input for future sessions.

Evaluating the Training Session Activity 7, Example 1

QUESTIONNAIRE: TST TRAINING EVALUATION

Name:.. Date:....................................
School:.. Position:..

Your help in completing this questionnaire will be most appreciated. Read each question and circle the answer provided which most closely fits what you believe. Please be as frank as you can with your answers. All questionnaires will be treated as strictly confidential and your identity will not be revealed.

IN ANSWERING THE FOLLOWING QUESTIONS, PLEASE TRY TO FOCUS SPECIFICALLY ON THE THREE TRAINING DAYS AND ACTIVITIES RATHER THAN ON INFORMATION YOU MAY PREVIOUSLY HAVE ACQUIRED.

1. How effective have the three training days been in familiarising you with the concept and principles of school-based TSTs as a means of providing peer support **and** meeting special educational needs?

    (not at all)   1   2   3   4   5   *(very)*

    Comment: ....
    ....

2. How well do you think the training has helped you understand the risks and constraints of designing and running a TST?

    (not at all)   1   2   3   4   5   *(very)*

    Comment: ....
    ....

3. How effective do you feel the training days have been in facilitating consultation with colleagues and designing an appropriate TST for your school?

    (not at all)   1   2   3   4   5   *(very)*

    Comment: ....
    ....

4. How effective has the training been in increasing your awareness and sensitivity to the needs and feelings of teachers requesting support?

    (not at all)   1   2   3   4   5   *(very)*

    Comment: ....
    ....

5. One of the longer term aims of training is for participating teachers to be proficient in the following areas (a to h). Taking the limitations imposed by such a short training period into account, how well do you feel the training days have prepared you for the following activities?

(a) Setting up a school-based TST

    (not at all)   1   2   3   4   5   *(very)*

    Comment: ....
    ....

(b) Receiving requests for support

    (not at all)   1   2   3   4   5   *(very)*

    Comment: ....
    ....

(c) Conducting meetings

    (not at all)   1   2   3   4   5   *(very)*

    Comment: ....
    ....

(d) Liaising with parents and support services

    (not at all)   1   2   3   4   5   *(very)*

Comment: ....
....

(e) Making sense of teaching problems

    (not at all)   1   2   3   4   5   *(very)*

Comment: ....
....

(f) Devising appropriate forms of advice

    (not at all)   1   2   3   4   5   *(very)*

Comment: ....
....

(g) Assessing outcomes in the classroom

    (not at all)   1   2   3   4   5   *(very)*

Comment: ....
....

(h) Reviewing and evaluating overall TST arrangements

    (not at all)   1   2   3   4   5   *(very)*

Comment: ....
....

6. Since opportunities for further training are available through the cross-school meetings, are there any of the above activities for which you still feel you need further support or training? Please specify.

....
....
....

7. How appropriate and effective was the level and amount of input from the trainers?

    (not at all)   1   2   3   4   5   *(very)*

Comment: ....
....

8. How appropriate was the pre-training literature as preparation for the training?

    (not at all)   1   2   3   4   5   *(very)*

Comment: ....
....

9. What in your opinion has been the **most** valuable or useful part of the training?

....
....

10. And what has been the **least** valuable or useful?

....
....

If you have any further comments which you would like to make about the content or quality of the training days, or if you have questions, ideas or issues which you feel it would be useful or important to raise at one of the next support meetings, please use this space.

....
....
....
....

THANK YOU FOR YOUR TIME AND EFFORT IN COMPLETING THIS QUESTIONNAIRE.

8 Providing Ongoing Support for your TST

Part of the ongoing support for TSTs must come from the teams themselves. Team members will need to reassess the technicalities of how the team operates, such as size of team, roles within the team, and rotating team membership (see Activity 2, Handout 1, page 24). Teams will also need to review their involvement with the senior management team as a means of continuously promoting the TST in the school. To this end, teams may wish to invite a senior teacher to be involved in the TST's own termly/annual review of its workings.

Another way of supporting the TST is to involve appropriate members of the Support Services. This support could come from Behaviour Support Services, Advisory Services or through the support of Educational Psychologists.

A final suggestion for providing ongoing support for TSTs is for clusters of schools involved in running TSTs to meet occasionally to exchange ideas and practices. In the TSTs already established in primary and secondary schools, one of the most helpful aspects of the training and ongoing support was felt to be the contact with colleagues from other schools doing similar work. TST members value the mutual support given by the regular meetings of networks of other schools running TSTs.

Given appropriate conditions within the school, TSTs can make a significant difference to the quality of teaching and learning. As one Deputy Head said:

> The TST ensures that the help is within the school, and therefore it is set in its proper context. It's not like so many other things which tell you what you **should** be doing – you should be differentiating your input, your output, your this, your that. It highlights the fact that we have expertise within the school. It will also highlight the fact that we are a team and teachers support each other.

Appendix – Past Studies

This appendix has two parts. The first reviews previous research on TSTs and the second offers the reader a list for further reading.

Peer Support Teams

Peer support teams have been discussed in a variety of professional contexts. Quality circles (Karp, 1983) are used in industry and have been developed in professional educational psychology (Fox, Pratt and Roberts, 1990). In the area of mental health consultation, the work of Caplan (1970) has been influential and has been extensively applied. Teacher-assistance teams – the origin of the TST idea – have been adopted and even mandated in some States of the USA (Ritter, 1978; Chalfant and Pysh, 1989; Graden, Casey and Christenson, 1985 a and b). In the USA, a Department of Education task force (Will, 1986) recommended that schools establish support systems for teachers as a way of responding to concerns about over-referral rates, misclassification of students, rising costs and the need to maximise opportunities for all students in the least restrictive environment (Chalfant and Pysh, 1989). The American research has indicated that TSTs can contribute to a drop in the number of inappropriate referrals to outside services (Chalfant and Pysh, 1989). As these authors point out, 'Fewer referrals make it possible for special education personnel to reallocate their time on other priorities' (page 53).

Supporting Teachers – Previous Studies

Surprisingly little work on support teams has been done in the UK. Instead, work has tended to focus on individual support teachers and SEN coordinators (Dyson, 1990; Garnett, 1988; Hart, 1986). The exception to this is the work of Hanko (1989, 1990), Mead (1991) and the Newcastle Educational Psychology Service (Stringer *et al.*, 1992). Hanko's focus is a school consultation and group support approach. Here, school consultation is led by outside professionals in a way which mirrors some of the American work. She has offered this as an approach to meet the recommendations for teacher peer support systems which were made in the Elton Report (DES, 1989, recommendation 6). Whereas Hanko acted as a group facilitator, Mead (1991) advocated task-orientated peer support groups (PSG) to increase the reflective nature of work in schools, thereby reducing teacher stress and increasing teacher effectiveness. PSGs were seen to provide forms of organisational structure that reinforced informal social support and resulted in greater feelings of ownership and personal competence. Chisholm (1994) reports a programme involving 55 schools over two years which drew on the concept of peer support to promote school-based development projects concerned with policy development, classroom approaches and co-teaching. This involved training a facilitator in each school whose role was to support the setting up and running of peer groups which undertook the projects. Evaluation showed that the group peer support system contributed to the success of the projects. What is interesting about the Mead and Chisholm studies is that both used peer support groups for development work and not for supporting individual teachers, as in TSTs. By contrast, the Newcastle Educational Psychology Service has been involved in training teachers to act in a support capacity to their colleagues.

Another line of inquiry is that which looks at the usefulness of teams as effective vehicles for change in schools (Henkin and Wanat, 1994). Theories of change in school settings argue that cultures of collaboration, rather than individualism, create and enhance 'qualities of openness, trust and support between teachers and their colleagues' (Hargreaves and Fullan, 1992, page 233). Collaborative cultures are ones which encourage learning from one another, by group problem-solving, sharing ideas and encouragement. Collaborative schools tend more often to be 'moving' schools rather than 'stuck' schools (Rosenholtz, 1991, page 149); moreover, collaborative schools develop educational expertise as a community.

Lack of time and opportunity (Nias, 1993, page 155) in schools makes it difficult for teachers to talk to one another about professional issues. TSTs can provide teachers with an opportunity both to talk and be listened to in the normally rushed environment of the school. In a current study on TSTs in secondary schools (DfEE, forthcoming) the teachers frequently mention the need for time and reflection. TSTs are seen as a way to formalise and recognise the need for such time. As two classroom teachers from schools in the secondary school research project said:

> As people get less time to listen to people I think that is one of the main things a TST can do. People can have time and get a chance to talk about something which is bothering them. Sometimes that just helps anyway. You do find that people are rushing about so much at the moment that they don't get time to listen. (Classroom teacher)

> I think it's always good for teachers to get together and talk about students' needs, and I think particularly since the introduction of the National Curriculum, people feel they don't have time. They're so busy, doing endless paperwork, it's actually having the time when you can sit down and say, 'This child needs talking about'. I think at that very simple level, it's a huge benefit, that it's a specific time when what you're talking about is children's needs and children's learning and how you teach, so I think from that point of view it's of great benefit. (Classroom teacher)

Schools need structures which allow them to face the challenges of change. TSTs can be seen as such a structure. TSTs allow teachers to support one another through these fast and uncertain times.

Recent and Current Research on TSTs in the UK

The outcomes of peer support in the schools studied are encouraging. Two recent studies, a pilot project in three primary schools (Daniels and Norwich, 1992) and an ESRC project in a further eight primary schools (Norwich and Daniels, 1994), looked at the processes and outcomes of the setting up of TSTs. Researchers and schools collaborated to evaluate the operation and impacts of TSTs at the schools. This involved collecting information about the frequency of the meetings, the number of requests, the nature of the concerns expressed, what action was recommended and what follow-up meetings were organised. This information was analysed within the context of each particular school with a view to understanding how a school's culture can contribute to supporting new schemes and how new schemes can contribute to a school's need to deal with and shape change. At the time of writing a DfEE research project is investigating the setting up and processes of TSTs in five secondary schools.

In the primary school projects mentioned above, the outcomes of the TST's work were positive. Teachers who were members of the team and teachers who referred to the team for help both reported that they felt their professional development was enhanced through the discussion and development of strategies – new, forgotten or known but not previously used – to deal with situations that were personally important to them at that time. These included:

- strategies for collaborating with other staff – this involved the direct involvement of the SEN coordinator or a TST member covering for a teacher;
- strategies for the teacher to use in-class – examples included the use of conduct charts, contracts and report books, the development of individual programmes and changes in class management such as the use of group work and seating rearrangements;
- strategies for lunchtime – for example play materials were made available to some pupils to encourage more constructive play;
- parental involvement – arranging specific meetings with parents and reaching agreement for parents to help their children in specific ways at home;
- communication with external support services – this involved writing to educational psychologists about statutory assessment or about bringing forward the date for the Statement review.

The TST members were very positive about the value of their TST work for themselves as teachers. All were keen to continue as members. For the SEN coordinator in particular, TSTs were seen as positively affecting their work by promoting linking across the school and preventing isolation.

Overall there were fewer requests in relation to girls than to boys, and to older than to younger children. At the end of a two-term period only a small proportion of the requests dealt with were judged as closed in the sense that improvement was sufficient to merit the withdrawal of support. However, there was some improvement in about two-thirds of the requests, as judged by the TSTs. In all schools the requesting teachers were mostly positive about the value for themselves of going to the team. The headteachers corroborated these views. Teachers' perceptions of the support offered to them by the TSTs included the following themes:

- enabled them to distance themselves from problems and re-examine their activities;
- enabled problems to be aired;
- enabled them to form their own strategies;
- opportunity to let off steam legitimately, it being cathartic to talk to sympathetic, non-judgemental colleagues;
- enabled them to confirm approaches already being used;
- opportunity to discuss school policy which could then be raised at staff meetings.

Below are examples of typical comments by teachers about TSTs:

'Staff feel now that they do not have to struggle on single-handed.'

'A joint approach to handling the child was agreed upon. There was open and frank dialogue with colleagues.'

'Teachers feel they are not alone with a problem. More people to share ideas with – more team spirit and sharing of experiences.'

In particular, the study showed how the TST supported teachers' perceptions of the difficulty of a situation. A validation of the teachers' perceptions led to an enhancement in the utility of their own intervention strategies, which were reaffirmed (Norwich and Daniels, 1994).

Reading List

Caplan, G. (1970) *Theory and practice of mental health consultation*. Basic Books.

Chalfant, J.C. and Pysh, M. (1989) 'Teacher assistance teams: five descriptive studies on 96 teams', *Remedial and Special Education*, 10, 6, 49–58.

Chisholm, B. (1994) 'Promoting peer support among teachers', in Gray, P., Miller, A. and Noakes, J. (eds) *Challenging behaviour in schools*. Routledge.

Daniels, H. and Norwich, B. (1992) *Teacher support teams: an interim evaluation report*. Institute of Education, London University.

DES (1989) *Discipline in schools* (Elton Report). HMSO.

DfE (1994) *Code of Practice on the Identification and Assessment of Special Educational Needs*. HMSO.

DfEE (forthcoming) *Provision of a teacher centred strategy for implementing the SEN Code of Practice*. Unpublished report.

Dyson, A. (1990) 'Effective learning consultancy: a future role for special needs co-ordinators', *Support for Learning*, 5, 3, 116–127.

Fox, M., Pratt, G. and Roberts, S. (1990) 'Developing the educational psychologists work in the secondary school: a process model for change', *Educational Psychology in Practice*, 6, 3, 163–169.

Galloway, D. (1985) *Schools, pupils and special educational needs*. Croom Helm.

Garnett, J. (1988) 'Support teaching: taking a closer look', *British Journal of Special Education*, 15, 1, 15–18.

Graden, J.L., Casey, A. and Christenson, S.L. (1985a) 'Implementing a pre-referral intervention system, Part 1: the model', *Exceptional Children*, 51, 377–384.

Graden, J.L., Casey, A. and Christenson, S.L. (1985b) 'Implementing a pre-referral intervention system, Part 2: the data', *Exceptional Children*, 51, 487–496.

Hanko, G. (1989) 'After Elton – how to manage disruption', *British Journal of Special Education*, 16, 4, 140–143.

Hanko, G. (1990) *Special needs in ordinary classrooms, supporting teachers*. Oxford: Blackwells/Third edition (1995) London: David Fulton Publishers.

Hart, S. (1986) 'Evaluating support teaching', *Gnosis*, 9, 26–32.

Hargreaves, A. and Fullan, M. (1992) *Understanding Teacher Development*. Cassell.

Henkin, A.B. and Wanat, C.L. (1994) 'Problem solving teams and the improvement of organizational performance in schools', *School Organisation*, 14, 2, 121–139.

ILEA (1985) *Equal opportunities for all?* (Fish Report). Inner London Education Authority.

Karp, H.B. (1983) *A Look at Quality Circles – 1983 Annual for Facilitators, Trainers and Consultants*. University Associates.

Mead, C. (1991) *A City-Wide Evaluation of PSG Training*. Birmingham Local Education Authority.

NCC (1989) *Circular No. 5*. National Curriculum Council.

Nias, J. (1993) 'Changing Times, Changing Identities: Grieving for a Lost Self', in Burgess, R. (ed.) *Educational Research & Evaluation for Policy and Practice*. Falmer Press.

Norwich, B. and Daniels, H. (1994) Evaluating teacher support teams: a strategy for special needs in ordinary schools. *ESRC Final Report – R-000-23-3859*. Unpublished.

Ritter, D.R. (1978) 'Effects of school consultation program on referral patterns of teachers', *Psychology in the Schools*, 15, 2, 239–243.

Rosenholtz, S. (1989) *Teachers' Workplace: The Social Organization of Schools*. White Plains, NY: Longman.

Stringer, P., Stow, L., Hibbert, K., Powell, J. and Louw, E. (1992) 'Establishing staff consultation groups in schools', *Educational Psychology in Practice*, 8, 2, 87–96.

Will, M. (1986) *Educating Students with Learning Problems: Shared Responsibility*. US Department for Education, Office of Special Education and Rehabilitation Services.